Stand up, Pam!

Pam needed to get her teeth
checked. So Mum and Nat
were off to the vet with her.

2

Pam loved to go on car trips.
Her ears flapped in the wind
and she gulped in the air.

Mum parked the car and Pam hopped out at high speed with her tail wagging.

4

Nat led Pam up to the Vet.
All of a sudden, Pam stopped
in fright and so did her tail!

Nat had to get her into the waiting room. As soon as she was in, Pam flopped down.

Mum frowned, "It seems Pam is not too keen on seeing the vet this morning."

It was Pam's turn. Mum
stood up and said,
"Come on, Pam. Stand
up! There's a good dog."

But Pam did not stand. Mum
and Nat attempted to pick
her up. But Pam was a big
dog and she was not helping.

The vet bent down next to Pam
and said, "What is the matter
Pam? This isn't like you."

The vet winked at Nat and said, "I think a little dog snack will do the trick."

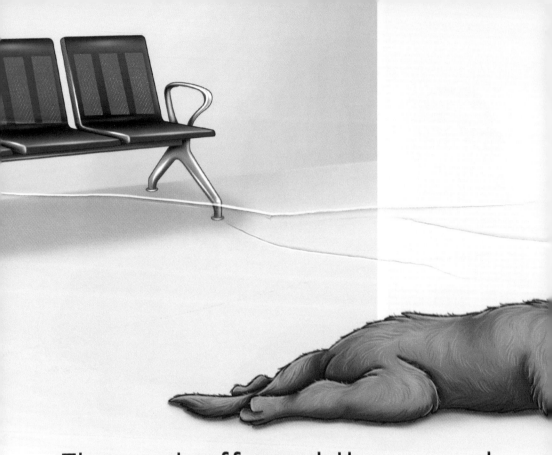

The vet offered the snack to Pam. Pam sniffed it and started to drool but she did not pick it up.

The vet said, "It looks like I will need to check your teeth here in the waiting room!"

The vet got a stool to sit on and looked at Pam's teeth. She said, "Your teeth are good Pam. You are free to go."

Pam jumped to her feet, shook herself and wagged her tail.

Then Pam grabbed the
packet of dog snacks and
ran off!

16

Words to blend

trips	flapped	wind
gulped	stopped	moving
flopped	stand	herself
grabbed	attempted	helping
bent	next	winked
snack	trick	sniffed
jumped	matter	packet

Before reading

Synopsis: Pam doesn't like going to the vet. Nothing Nat or Mum do can make Pam stand up so the vet can look at her teeth.

Review graphemes/phonemes: oo ar ow ee igh

Book discussion: Look at the cover and read the title together. Ask: *What is Pam doing in the cover picture? Where do you think this story is set? What might happen?*

Link to prior learning: Display a word with adjacent consonants from the story, e.g. *started*. Ask the children to put a dot under the single-letter graphemes (*s, t, t, e, d*) and a line under the digraph (*ar*). Model, if necessary, how to sound out and blend the sounds together to read the word. Repeat with another word from the story, e.g. *stool*, and encourage the children to sound out and blend the word independently.

Vocabulary check: gulped – swallowed noisily

Decoding practice: Display the word *frowned*. Focus on the *ed* at the end, and remind children that in some words, these two letters make a /d/ sound at the end of the word. Sound out and blend all through the word: f-r-ow-n-d.

Tricky word practice: Display the word *all* and ask children to point out the tricky parts of the word (*a*, which makes the /or/ sound. Ask children to find and read the word in the book. Practise writing and reading the word.

After reading

Apply learning: Ask: *How did Pam feel when she first got to the vet's? How did she feel at the end? What caused the difference?* (She was scared/uncooperative at first, but at the end she was much happier because the visit to the vet was over, and she had some snacks.)

Comprehension

- Who takes Pam to the vet?

- Why does Pam need to go there?

- Where does the vet check Pam's teeth?

Fluency

- Pick a page that most of the group read quite easily. Ask them to reread it with pace and expression. Model how to do this if necessary.

- Ask children to turn to page 8 and read Mum's speech with lots of expression, so it sounds as if she is really talking.

- Practise reading the words on page 17.

Tricky words review

to	so	were
all	go	she
loved	come	said
what	like	you
little	your	here